little book of

Rum

Cocktails

little book of
Rum
Cocktails

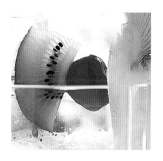

hamlyn

First published in 2000 by Hamlyn
an imprint of Octopus Publishing Group Limited
2–4 Heron Quays, London E14 4JP

British Library Cataloguing-in-Publication Data
A catalogue record for this book is available from the British Library

ISBN 0 600 60143 9

Printed in China

Notes for American readers

The measure that has been used in the recipes is
based on a bar jigger, which is 45 ml (1½ fl oz). If
preferred, a different volume can be used providing
the proportions are kept constant within a drink and
suitable adjustments are made to spoon
measurements, where they occur.

Standard level spoon measurements are used in all
recipes.
1 tablespoon = one 15 ml spoon
1 teaspoon = one 5 ml spoon
Imperial and metric measurements have been given
in some of the recipes. Use one set of measurements
only and not a mixture of both.

UK	US
caster sugar	granulated sugar
cocktail cherries	maraschino cherries
cocktail stick	toothpick
double cream	heavy cream
drinking chocolate	presweetened cocoa powder
icing sugar	confectioners' sugar
jug	pitcher
lemon rind	lemon peel or zest
single cream	light cream
soda water	club soda

Contents

Introduction

Rum has a strange mixture of associations – from smugglers risking shipwreck off the Cornish coast and capture by the merciless militia men, or as the free tipple that kept the British Navy happy, to wealthy planters relaxing on sunny verandas leisurely sipping long fruit-bedecked concoctions.

Christopher Columbus is said to have introduced sugar cane to the Caribbean. While this may be mere legend, it is undoubtedly true that the Caribbean introduced the rest of the world to the spirit distilled from it – rum. By the 17th century distillation from sugar cane or its products was taking place in Hispaniola to produce a spirit that a contemporary described as 'hot, hellish and terrible'.

Over the years, it became more palatable, as new techniques were discovered –

cultured yeasts, the benefit of maturing in casks, improved filtration and, in the 1830s, the patent still. From being a rough spirit that only colonists drank for want of anything better, it became a popular drink, first in western Europe and later throughout the world. The right of sailors to a rum ration was enshrined by Britain's Royal Navy and was not abolished until the 20th century.

Rum is distilled from molasses and, in some cases, directly from the fermented juices of the sugar cane. To begin with, it is a colourless, high-strength spirit with little natural flavour. Caramel may then be added to give colour and some premium rums also acquire colour while maturing in oak casks. There are basically three types of rum – white, golden or light and dark. Various flavourings are also added and it is common for rums from different places to be blended.

Rum is produced wherever sugar cane grows, but, arguably, the Caribbean produces the best and each island group has its own type. Martinique and Jamaica are well-known for pungent, sweet, heavy-bodied dark rums. Paler, drier and lighter golden rums are widely produced, especially in Cuba, Puerto Rico and Barbados. Puerto Rico is also the largest producer of white rum, but it is made in many other places, too.

White rum is a popular base for cocktails, as it blends easily with a wide range of flavours. Many classics – Daiquiri, Piña Colada, Blue Hawaiian and Mai Tai – are white rum cocktails. Darker rums combine superbly with fruit juices, especially lime, and are perfect for cold or hot punches. Some cocktails, such as the Zombie, are based on a mixture of different types of rum and, perhaps surprisingly, although it has a strong flavour itself, rum combines well with other spirits and liqueurs.

Sugar Syrup

This may be used instead of sugar to sweeten cocktails and to give them more body. It can be bought, but is simple to make at home.

Put 4 tablespoons of sugar and 4 tablespoons water in a small pan and stir over a low heat until the sugar has dissolved. Bring to the boil and boil, without stirring, for 1–2 minutes. Store in a sterilized bottle in the refrigerator for up to 2 months.

Daiquiris & Zombies

9

Daiquiri

cracked ice
juice of 2 limes
1 teaspoon sugar syrup
   (see page 7)
3 measures white rum

The Daiquiri was created by an American mining engineer working in Cuba in 1896. He was expecting VIP guests and his supplies of gin had run out, so he extemporized with rum – and created this classic cocktail.

Put lots of cracked ice into a cocktail shaker. Pour the lime juice, sugar syrup and rum over the ice. Shake thoroughly until a frost forms, then strain into a chilled cocktail glass.

Serves 1

Banana Daiquiri

3 ice cubes, cracked
2 measures white rum
½ measure banana
    liqueur
½ small banana
½ measure lime cordial

to decorate
1 teaspoon powdered
    sugar (optional)
slice of banana

Put the cracked ice in a margarita glass or tall goblet. Put the rum, banana liqueur, banana and lime cordial into a blender and blend for 30 seconds. Pour into the glass and decorate with the powdered sugar, if using, and banana slice.

Serves 1

Apricot Daiquiri

crushed ice
1 measure white rum
1 measure lemon juice
½ measure apricot liqueur
    or brandy
3 ripe apricots, peeled
    and pitted

to decorate
slice of apricot
cocktail cherry
mint sprig

This pretty pale-coloured cocktail looks particularly attractive if it is decorated by cutting the apricot slice in half and spearing the two halves and the cocktail cherry with a cocktail stick. Balance the cocktail stick across the glass on the rim.

Put some crushed ice into a blender. Add the rum, lemon juice, apricot liqueur or brandy and the apricots and blend for 1 minute, or until the mixture is smooth. Pour into a chilled cocktail glass and decorate with an apricot slice, a cocktail cherry and mint sprig.

Serves 1

Coconut Daiquiri

crushed ice
2 measures coconut
    liqueur
2 measures fresh
    lime juice
1 measure white rum
1 dash egg white
slice of lime, to decorate

Put the ice in a cocktail shaker
and add all the ingredients.
Shake vigorously until a frost
forms. Strain and pour into a
chilled cocktail glass. Decorate
with a slice of lime.

Serves 1

Strawberry Daiquiri

1 measure white rum
½ measure crème
    de fraises
½ measure fresh
    lemon juice
4 ripe strawberries,
    hulled
crushed ice

to decorate
slice of strawberry
mint sprig

This fruity cocktail is especially delicious if you make it with crème de fraises des bois, a wild strawberry liqueur.

Put the rum, crème de fraises, lemon juice, strawberries and ice into a food processor or blender and process at a slow speed for 5 seconds, then at high speed for about 20 seconds. Pour into a chilled glass and decorate with a strawberry slice and a mint sprig.

Serves 1

Frozen Pineapple Daiquiri

crushed ice
2–3 pineapple slices
½ measure fresh
    lime juice
1 measure white rum
¼ measure Cointreau
1 teaspoon sugar syrup
    (see page 7)
piece of pineapple,
    to decorate

Put some crushed ice into a blender and add the pineapple slices, lime juice, white rum, Cointreau and sugar syrup. Blend at the highest speed until smooth, then pour into a chilled cocktail glass. Decorate with a piece of fresh pineapple and serve with straw.

Serves 1

Melon Daiquiri

2 measures white rum
1 measure fresh
    lime juice
2 dashes Midori liqueur
2 scoops crushed ice

Put the white rum, lime juice and liqueur in a blender with the crushed ice and blend until smooth. Serve in a chilled goblet with straws.

Serves 1

Havana Zombie

4–5 ice cubes
juice of 1 lime
5 tablespoons
    pineapple juice
1 teaspoon sugar syrup
    (see page 7)
1 measure white rum
1 measure golden rum
1 measure dark rum

Put the ice cubes into a mixing glass. Pour the lime juice, pineapple juice, sugar syrup and rums over the ice and stir vigorously. Pour, without straining, into a tall glass.

Serves 1

Zombie

3 ice cubes, cracked
1 measure dark rum
1 measure white rum
½ measure golden rum
½ measure apricot brandy
juice of ½ lime
2 measures
    unsweetened
    pineapple juice
2 teaspoons powdered
    sugar

to decorate
slice of kiwi fruit
cocktail cherry
pineapple wedge
powdered sugar
    (optional)

Zombies contain all three types of rum – dark, golden and white. The darker rums are aged in charred oak casks while white rums are aged in stainless steel tanks.

Place a tall glass in the freezer so the outside becomes frosted. Put the ice into a cocktail shaker. Add the rums, apricot brandy, lime juice, pineapple juice and sugar. Shake to mix. Pour into the glass without straining. To decorate, spear the slice of kiwi fruit, cherry and pineapple with a cocktail stick and place it across the top of the glass, balanced on the rim. Sprinkle the powdered sugar over the top and serve.

Serves 1

Zombie Christophe

4–5 ice cubes
juice of 1 lime or lemon
juice of ½ orange
250 ml (8 fl oz)
    unsweetened
    pineapple juice
1 measure blue Curaçao
1 measure white rum
1 measure golden rum
½ measure dark rum

to decorate
slice of lime or lemon
mint sprig

Put the ice cubes into a mixing glass. Pour the lime or lemon juice, orange juice, pineapple juice, Curaçao, white and golden rums over the ice. Stir vigorously, then pour, without straining, into a tumbler. Top with the dark rum, stir gently and serve decorated with a slice of lime or lemon and a mint sprig.

Serves 1

Zombie Prince

crushed ice
juice of 1 lemon
juice of 1 orange
juice of ½ grapefruit
3 drops Angostura bitters
1 teaspoon soft
    brown sugar
1 measure white rum
1 measure golden rum
1 measure dark rum

to decorate
slices of lime
slices of orange

Put the crushed ice into a mixing glass. Pour the lemon, orange and grapefruit juices over the ice and splash in the bitters. Add the sugar and pour in the three rums. Stir vigorously, then pour, without straining, into a Collins glass. Decorate with slices of lime and orange.

Tip
A Collins glass is perfect for long drinks – the taller the better. They are always narrow with slightly tapered or perfectly straight sides.

Exotic Cocktails

Astronaut

Acapulco

Piña Colada

Coco Loco

Blue Hawaiian

Grenada

Mai Tai

Summertime

Banana Royal

Port Antonio

St Lucia

Bahamas

Serenade

Discovery Bay

Pussyfoot

Virgin's Prayer

Bombay Smash

Tropical Dream

Astronaut

8–10 ice cubes
½ measure white rum
½ measure vodka
½ measure lemon juice
1 dash passion fruit juice
lemon wedge, to
    decorate

Put 4–5 ice cubes into a cocktail shaker and add the rum, vodka, lemon and passion fruit juices. Fill an old-fashioned glass with 4–5 fresh ice cubes. Shake the cocktail until a frost forms, then strain it into the glass. Decorate with the lemon wedge.

Serves 1

Acapulco

crushed ice
1 measure tequila
1 measure white rum
2 measures
    pineapple juice
1 measure
    grapefruit juice
1 measure coconut milk
pineapple wedge,
    to decorate

Whenever a cocktail includes fruit juice, it always tastes better if the juice is freshly squeezed. Juice from a bottle or carton is better than nothing and the cocktail will still taste good.

Put some crushed ice into a cocktail shaker and pour in the tequila, rum, pineapple juice, grapefruit juice and coconut milk. Shake until a frost forms, then pour into a hurricane glass and decorate with a pineapple wedge. Serve with straws.

Serves 1

Piña Colada

cracked ice
1 measure white rum
2 measures coconut milk
(see opposite)
2 measures
pineapple juice

to decorate
slice of strawberry
slice of mango
slice of pineapple

Put some cracked ice, the rum,
coconut milk and pineapple juice
into a cocktail shaker. Shake
lightly to mix. Strain into a large
glass and decorate with the slices
of strawberry, mango and
pineapple.

Serves 1

Coco Loco

crushed ice
4 measures
   coconut water
1 measure coconut milk
1 measure apricot brandy
1 measure white rum
ground cinnamon

Coconut water is the thin liquid found inside a fresh coconut, whereas coconut milk is made by blending fresh coconut, grated coconut cream or desiccated coconut with hot water. Both coconut water and coconut milk are sold in cans.

Put some crushed ice into a blender and add the coconut water, coconut milk, apricot brandy and rum and blend at high speed. To serve, pour into a coconut shell and sprinkle with ground cinnamon.

Serves 1

Blue Hawaiian

crushed ice
1 measure white rum
½ measure blue Curaçao
2 measures
    pineapple juice
1 measure
    coconut cream
pineapple wedge,
    to decorate

The beautiful colour of this cocktail comes from the blue Curaçao, but the liqueur is actually made from bitter oranges.

Put some crushed ice into a blender and pour in the rum, blue Curaçao, pineapple juice and coconut cream. Blend at high speed for 20–30 seconds. Pour into a chilled cocktail glass and decorate with a pineapple wedge.

Serves 1

Grenada

4–5 ice cubes
juice of ½ orange
1 measure
    sweet vermouth
3 measures golden or
    dark rum
ground cinnamon

Put the ice cubes into a mixing glass. Pour the orange juice, vermouth and rum over the ice. Stir vigorously, then strain into a chilled cocktail glass. Sprinkle a little ground cinnamon on top.

Serves 1

Mai Tai

lightly beaten egg white
caster sugar, for frosting
1 measure white rum
½ measure orange juice
½ measure lime juice
3 ice cubes, crushed

to decorate
cocktail cherries
pineapple cubes
slice of orange

The name of this cocktail is taken from Tahitian and means good – it certainly is.

Dip the rim of a tall glass into the beaten egg white, then into the caster sugar. Put the rum, orange juice and lime juice into a cocktail shaker. Shake to mix. Put the ice into the glass and pour the cocktail over it. Decorate with the cherries, pineapple and a slice of orange and serve with a straw.

Serves 1

Summertime

3 ice cubes, cracked
1½ measures Grand
    Marnier or Cointreau
½ measure dark rum
2 teaspoons lemon juice
slice of lemon, to
    decorate

Both Cointreau and Grand Marnier are French liqueurs flavoured with oranges. Cointreau is a clear liquid, while Grand Marnier is brandy-based.

Put the ice cubes into a cocktail shaker and add the Grand Marnier or Cointreau, rum and lemon juice. Shake well. Strain into a cocktail glass and decorate with the slice of lemon.

Serves 1

Banana Royal

crushed ice
1½ measures coconut
    milk (see page 35)
3 measures
    pineapple juice
1½ measures golden rum
½ measure double cream
1 ripe banana
grated coconut,
    to decorate

Put some crushed ice into a blender and add the coconut milk, pineapple juice, rum, cream and banana. Blend at high speed for 15–30 seconds, until smooth and creamy. Pour into an old-fashioned glass and sprinkle with grated coconut.

Serves 1

Port Antonio

½ teaspoon grenadine
4–5 ice cubes
1 measure fresh
    lime juice
3 measures white rum or
    golden rum

to decorate
lime rind
cocktail cherry

Grenadine is a sweet non-alcoholic syrup made from pomegranates, which give it its rich rosy pink colour.

Spoon the grenadine into a chilled cocktail glass. Put the ice cubes into a mixing glass. Pour the lime juice and rum over the ice and stir vigorously, then strain into the cocktail glass. Wrap the lime rind round the cocktail cherry, spear them with a cocktail stick and use to decorate the drink.

Serves 1

St Lucia

4–5 ice cubes
1 measure Curaçao
1 measure dry vermouth
juice of ½ orange
1 teaspoon grenadine
2 measures white or
    golden rum

to decorate
orange rind spiral
cocktail cherry

Put the ice cubes into a cocktail shaker. Pour the Curaçao, dry vermouth, orange juice, grenadine and rum over the ice. Shake until a frost forms, then pour, without straining, into a highball glass. Decorate with an orange rind spiral and a cocktail cherry.

Serves 1

Bahamas

4–5 ice cubes
1 measure white rum
1 measure Southern
    Comfort
1 measure fresh
    lemon juice
1 dash crème de banane
thin lemon slice,
    to decorate

Put some ice cubes into a cocktail shaker and pour in the rum, Southern Comfort, lemon juice and crème de banane. Shake vigorously, then strain into a chilled cocktail glass. Drop in a thin lemon slice and serve.

Serves 1

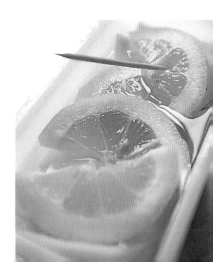

Serenade

6 ice cubes, crushed
1 measure white rum
½ measure Amaretto di
    Saronno
½ measure
    coconut cream
2 measures
    pineapple juice
slice of pineapple,
    to decorate

Amaretto is a sweet Italian liqueur made from apricot kernels, flavoured with almonds and herbs.

Put half of the ice into a blender and add the rum, Amaretto, coconut cream and pineapple juice and blend for 20 seconds. Put the remaining ice into a tall glass and pour the cocktail over it. Decorate with a slice of pineapple and drink with a straw.

Serves 1

Discovery Bay

4–5 ice cubes
3 drops Angostura bitters
juice of ½ lime
1 teaspoon Curaçao or
    blue Curaçao
1 teaspoon sugar syrup
    (see page 7)
3 measures golden or
    dark rum
lime slices, to decorate

**Curaçao comes from the
Dutch Caribbean island of
that name. It is produced in
several colours including a
vivid blue and honey-gold.**

Put the ice cubes into a cocktail
shaker. Shake the bitters over the
ice. Pour in the lime juice,
Curaçao, sugar syrup and rum
and shake until a frost forms.
Strain into an old fashioned
glass. Decorate with lime slices.

Serves 1

Pussyfoot

crushed ice
1½ measures white rum
1 measure double cream
1 measure
   pineapple juice
1 measure lime juice
1 measure cherry juice

to decorate
slice of pineapple
cocktail cherry

Although there is a well-known non-alcoholic cocktail called Pussyfoot, this more potent version, with a generous measure of rum, is something of a lion's paw.

Put some crushed ice into a blender and add the rum, cream, pineapple juice, lime juice and cherry juice. Blend at high speed for 15–20 seconds, then pour into a hurricane glass. Decorate with a slice of pineapple and a cherry.

Serves 1

Virgin's Prayer

ice
2 measures light rum
2 measures dark rum
2 measures Kahlua
2 tablespoons
    lemon juice
4 tablespoons
    orange juice
2 slices of lime, to
    decorate

Put some ice in a cocktail shaker
and pour in the rums, Kahlua,
lemon juice and orange juice and
shake until a frost forms. Strain
the cocktail into 2 rocks or
highball glasses and decorate
with the slices of lime.

Serves 2

Tip
Kahlua is a coffee
flavoured liqueur from
Mexico

Bombay Smash

5 ice cubes, crushed
1 measure dark rum
1 measure Malibu
3 measures
    pineapple juice
2 teaspoons lemon juice
¼ measure Cointreau

to decorate
pineapple cubes
slice of lemon

Put half of the ice into a cocktail shaker. Add the rum, Malibu, pineapple juice, lemon juice and Cointreau. Shake until a frost forms. Put the remaining ice into a tall glass and strain over the cocktail. Decorate with the pineapple cubes and slice of lemon and drink with a straw.

Serves 1

Tropical Dream

1 measure white rum

1 measure Midori

1 tablespoon coconut
    cream

1 tablespoon
    pineapple juice

3 tablespoons
    orange juice

3–4 ice cubes

½ measure crème
    de banane

½ fresh banana

wedge of fresh banana,
    with skin on,
    to decorate

Pour the white rum, Midori,
coconut cream, pineapple juice,
orange juice and the ice cubes
into a blender. Blend for about
10 seconds. Add the crème de
banane and the fresh banana and
blend for a further 10 seconds.
Decorate with the wedge of
banana and drink with a straw.

Serves 1

Punches & Fizzes

Florida Skies

cracked ice
1 measure white rum
¼ measure lime juice
½ measure
   pineapple juice
soda water, to top up
slices of cucumber or
   lime, to decorate

**For a Florida Hurricane, add
1 measure Curaçao and
substitute orange juice for
the pineapple juice. For a
Florida, add ½ measure
crème de menthe and
decorate with a mint sprig.**

Put some cracked ice in a tall
glass. Put the rum, lime and
pineapple juices into a cocktail
shaker. Shake lightly. Strain into
the glass and top up with soda
water. Decorate with the slices of
cucumber or lime.

Serves 1

Havana Beach

½ lime
2 measures
    pineapple juice
1 measure white rum
1 teaspoon sugar
ginger ale, to top up
slice of lime, to decorate

A hurricane glass is so called because it is shaped like a hurricane lamp. It is ideal for long drinks.

Cut the lime into 4 pieces and place in a blender with the pineapple juice, rum and sugar. Blend until smooth. Pour into a hurricane glass or large goblet and top up with ginger ale. Decorate with a slice of lime.

Serves 1

Cuba Libre

2–3 ice cubes
1½ measures dark rum
juice of ½ lime
cola, to top up
lime slice, to decorate

Place the ice cubes in a tall tumbler and pour over the rum and lime juice. Stir to mix. Top up with cola, decorate with a lime slice and drink through a straw.

Serves 1

Mississippi Punch

crushed ice
3 drops Angostura bitters
1 teaspoon sugar syrup
   (see page 7)
juice of 1 lemon
1 measure brandy
1 measure dark rum
2 measures bourbon or
   Scotch whisky

Fill a highball glass with crushed ice. Shake the bitters over the ice and pour in the sugar syrup and lemon juice. Stir gently to mix thoroughly. Add the brandy, rum and whisky, in that order, stir once and serve with drinking straws.

Serves 1

Bahamas Punch

juice of 1 lemon
1 teaspoon sugar syrup
    (see page 7)
3 drops Angostura bitters
½ teaspoon grenadine
3 measures white or
    golden rum
slice of orange
slice of lemon
cracked ice
grated nutmeg,
    to decorate

For Planter's Punch, substitute lime juice for the lemon juice, a slice of lime for the lemon slice, increase the quantity of grenadine to 1 teaspoon and use dark rum.

Pour the lemon juice and sugar syrup into a mixing glass. Shake in the bitters, then add the grenadine, rum and slices of orange and lemon. Stir thoroughly and chill in the refrigerator for 3 hours. To serve, fill an old-fashioned glass with cracked ice, pour in the punch, without straining, and sprinkle with nutmeg.

Serves 1

Pink Rum

3 drops Angostura bitters

3–4 ice cubes

2 measures white rum

2 measures
   cranberry juice

1 measure soda water

slice of lime, to decorate

Angostura bitters is a herb-flavoured essence used in small quantities to add flavour to drinks. Details of the recipe are a closely kept secret. Orange bitters are another favourite.

Shake the bitters into a highball glass and swirl them around. Add the ice cubes, then pour in the rum, cranberry juice and soda water and serve decorated with a slice of lime.

Serves 1

Tobago Fizz

4–5 ice cubes
juice of ½ lime or lemon
juice of ½ orange
3 measures golden rum
1 measure single cream
½ teaspoon sugar syrup
    (see page 7)
soda water, to top up

to decorate
slice of orange
slice of strawberry

Put the ice cubes into a cocktail shaker. Pour the lime or lemon juice, orange juice, rum, cream and sugar syrup over the ice. Shake until a frost forms, then strain into a goblet. Top with soda water and serve decorated with slices of orange and strawberry speared on a cocktail stick and drink with straws.

Serves 1

New Orleans Dandy

crushed ice
1 measure light rum
½ measure peach brandy
1 dash orange juice
1 dash lime juice
Champagne to top up

Place the crushed ice in a cocktail shaker with the rum, peach brandy, orange juice and lime juice. Shake until a frost forms. Strain into a large wine glass and top up with Champagne.

Serves 1

Pink Treasure

2 ice cubes, cracked
1 measure white rum
1 measure cherry brandy
bitter lemon or soda
    water (optional)
twist of lemon,
    to decorate

Put the ice cubes, rum and cherry brandy into a small glass. Add a splash of bitter lemon or soda water. Decorate with the twist of lemon.

Serves 1

Punch Julien

juice of 2 limes
1 measure
     pineapple juice
3 drops Angostura bitters
½ teaspoon grenadine
1 measure golden rum
3 measures dark rum
slice of lime
slice of lemon
slice of orange
cracked ice

to decorate
grated nutmeg
1 pineapple wedge

Pour the lime juice and pineapple juice into a mixing glass and shake in the bitters. Pour in the grenadine and golden and dark rums and add the fruit. Stir thoroughly, then chill in the refrigerator for 3 hours. Fill an old-fashioned glass with cracked ice. Pour the punch over the ice and add the fruit. Sprinkle with nutmeg and serve decorated with a pineapple wedge.

Serves 1

Golden Rum Punch

50 g (2 oz) sugar
1 litre (1¾ pints)
    pineapple juice
juice of 6 oranges
juice of 6 lemons
1 bottle golden rum
ice
1 litre (1¾ pints) ginger
    ale or soda water

to decorate
slices of fruit in season,
    such as pineapples,
    oranges, cherries and
    strawberries

Put the sugar into a punch bowl, pour in the pineapple juice and stir to dissolve the sugar. Add the orange and lemon juices and pour in the rum. Stir to mix. Put a large block of ice into the punch bowl and leave the punch to get really cold.

When you are ready to serve, pour in the ginger ale or soda water. Decorate with slices of pineapple and orange, cherries, strawberries and any other fruit in season.

Serves 20

Slow Sippers

Alexander Baby

Black Widow

Rum Martini

Honeysuckle

Batiste

White Witch

Heartwarmer

Between the Sheets

Sunset Tea

Island Cream Grog

Alexander Baby

slow sippers

4–5 ice cubes
2 measures dark rum
1 measure crème
     de cacao
½ measure double cream
grated nutmeg,
     to decorate

This is the younger – but no less powerful – brother of the classic gin- and brandy-based cocktails, Alexander and Brandy Alexander.

Put the ice cubes into a cocktail shaker and pour the rum, crème de cacao and cream over it. Shake a frost forms, then strain it into a chilled cocktail glass. Sprinkle grated nutmeg on top.

Serves 1

Tip

Crème de cacao is a chocolate-flavoured liqueur which comes in colourless and chocolate-brown varieties.

Black Widow

4–5 ice cubes
2 measures dark rum
1 measure Southern
    Comfort
juice of ½ lime
1 dash sugar syrup (see
    page 7)
slice of lime, to decorate

Put the ice cubes into a cocktail shaker. Pour in the dark rum, Southern Comfort, lime juice and sugar syrup and shake until a frost forms. Strain into a chilled cocktail glass and decorate with a slice of lime.

Serves 1

Rum Martini

4–5 ice cubes
1 measure dry vermouth
3 measures white rum
1 piece of lemon rind

Put the ice cubes into a mixing glass. Pour the vermouth and rum over the ice, stir vigorously, then strain into a chilled cocktail glass. Twist the lemon rind over the drink and drop it in.

Serves 1

Honeysuckle

4–5 ice cubes
2 measures golden rum
juice of 1 lime
1 teaspoon clear honey

This cocktail is especially flavoursome when made with lemon or orange blossom honey.

Put the ice cubes into a cocktail shaker. Pour in the rum and lime juice and add the honey. Shake until a frost forms, then strain into a cocktail glass.

Serves 1

Batiste

4–5 ice cubes
1 measure
   Grand Marnier
2 measures golden or
   dark rum

Grand Marnier is a brandy-based orange liqueur. It is made by a French liqueur company, hence its presence in this cocktail which comes from one of the French-speaking islands in the Caribbean.

Put the ice cubes into a mixing glass. Pour the Grand Marnier and rum over the ice, stir vigorously, then strain into a cocktail glass.

Serves 1

White Witch

8–10 ice cubes
1 measure white rum
½ measure white crème
    de cacao
½ measure Cointreau
juice of ½ lime
soda water, to top up

to decorate
slice of orange
slice of lime

Put 4–5 ice cubes into a cocktail shaker and pour in the rum, crème de cacao, Cointreau and lime juice. Put 4–5 fresh ice cubes into an old-fashioned glass. Shake the drink, then strain it into the glass. Top up with soda water and stir to mix. Decorate with slices of orange and lime and serve with straws.

Serves 1

Tip

If you roll whole limes around quite hard on a board with your hand, you will find that you get more juice from them.

Heartwarmer

200 ml (7 fl oz) red
    grape juice
250 g (8 oz) brown sugar
350 ml (12 fl oz) dark rum
1.5 litres (2½ pints) dry
    white wine
450 ml (¾ pint) red wine

Put the grape juice into a saucepan, add the sugar and stir over a gentle heat until the sugar has dissolved completely. Stir in the dark rum and set aside. Pour the white wine and red wine into a large saucepan and heat until hot, but not boiling. Add the rum and grape juice mixture and stir together. Serve hot.

Serves 12

Between the Sheets

4–5 ice cubes
1¼ measures brandy
1 measure white rum
½ measure Cointreau
¾ measure lemon juice
½ measure sugar syrup
(see page 7)

Put the ice cubes into a cocktail shaker. Add the brandy, white rum, Cointreau, lemon juice and sugar syrup and shake until a frost forms. Strain into a chilled cocktail glass.

Serves 1

Sunset Tea

slow sippers

200 ml (7 fl oz) freshly
    brewed Indian tea
½ measure golden rum
1 measure Cointreau
2 measures orange juice

to decorate
2 slices of orange, each
    stuck with 3 cloves
cinnamon sticks

Pour the tea into 2 heatproof glasses. Put the rum, Cointreau and orange juice into a small saucepan. Place it over a low heat and bring the mixture to just under boiling point, stirring constantly. Pour immediately into the glasses with the tea. Decorate with a slice of orange stuck with 3 cloves, and a cinnamon stick.

Serves 2

Island Cream Grog

2 measures rum
200 ml (7 fl oz) boiling
    water
sugar to taste
whipped cream
grated nutmeg

For Hot Buttered Rum, stir 15 g (½ oz) butter with the rum before adding the boiling water and omit the whipped cream.

Warm a heatproof glass with a handle and pour in the rum and boiling water. Add sugar to taste and stir. Spoon some whipped cream on top and sprinkle with grated nutmeg.

Serves 1

INDEX

Acknowledgements

Octopus Publishing Group
  Ltd./David Loftus 91
  /Neil Mersh 11, 13, 17, 25, 26,
  28, 39, 41, 51, 57, 58, 63,
  67, 69, 71, 75, 87
  /Peter Myers 8, 64
  /William Reavell Cover, 2, 3, 5,
  6-7, 15, 19, 20, 22, 31, 33,
  34, 37, 43, 45, 47, 48, 53,
  55, 61, 73, 77, 78, 81, 83,
  84, 89, 93, 95